CONTENTS

A duck starts life inside an egg. In spring, the female duck lays her eggs beside a pond. She makes a nest from grass and leaves. She lines it with warm, fluffy feathers.

ANIMALS AND THEIR BABIES
Ducks and Ducklings

written by Anita Ganeri

illustrated by Anni Axworthy

A Cherrytree book

Published by
Evans Publishing Group
2A Portman Mansions
Chiltern St
London W1U 6NR

First published in 2007

Printed in China by WKT Co Ltd

British Library Cataloguing in Publication Data
Ganeri, Anita, 1961-
   Ducks and ducklings. - (Animals and their babies)
   1. Ducklings - Juvenile literature 2. Ducks - Life cycles -
   Juvenile literature
   I. Title
   598.4'1156

ISBN 978184 234444 6

The female lays an egg every day or two until there are about 12 eggs. The male duck chases other ducks away so that they do not harm the eggs. Then he swims away.

The mother duck sits on the eggs to keep them warm. This helps the baby ducks inside to grow. The mother duck only gets up to find food and stretch her legs.

Animals such as foxes like to eat duck eggs.
The mother duck's speckled brown feathers
match the colour of the ground. This helps
to hide the mother duck and the nest.

9

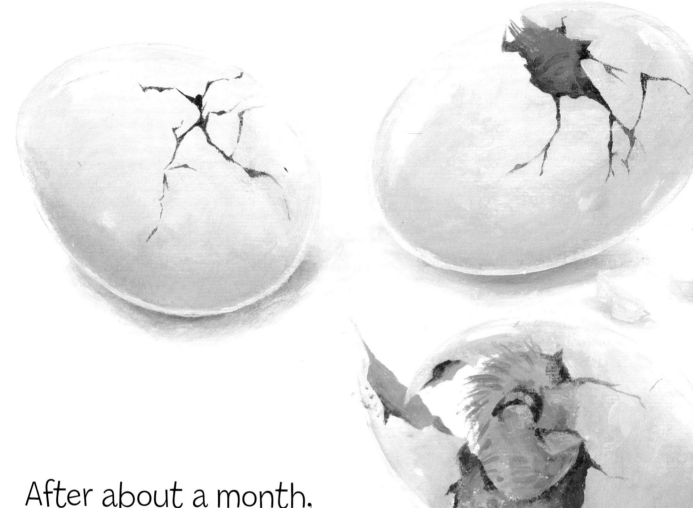

After about a month,
the baby ducks are ready
to hatch out of their eggs.
Each baby duck chips a hole in
the eggshell with its sharp little beak.

Baby ducks are called ducklings. They are covered in soft, fluffy feathers called down. They cheep as they come out of their eggs.

The new ducklings are very hungry. About 12 hours after hatching from their eggs, they are ready to leave their nest to find food.

Their mother leads the ducklings to the pond
for their first swim. They have webbed feet
for paddling through the water.
They swim close to their mother.

The mother duck shows the ducklings what they can eat. They eat seeds and water plants, snails, insects and shellfish.

The ducklings scoop up some of their food from the surface of the water. They also reach under the water to find plants to eat.

Young ducklings are sometimes eaten by fish and birds. If the mother duck sees danger, she gives a loud 'quack' to the ducklings to come to her.

At night, the ducklings snuggle up under their mother's wings. This helps to keep them safe and warm if the weather turns cold.

When the ducklings are about two months old, they are ready to learn to fly.

First, they have to practise flapping their wings.

Ducks are fast, strong fliers. They fly with other ducks in big groups called flocks. They flap their wings to take off from the water and spread their wings out to land.

The duckling is a year old.
It is now a grown-up duck.

A male duck usually has brightly
coloured feathers. A female duck
has plain brown feathers.

The duck is old enough to have its own ducklings.
In autumn, a male and female duck meet up.
Next spring, the female duck lays her eggs.
And the eggs hatch into . . . new ducklings!

Index

Further Information

The ducks featured in this book are mallards (Anas platyrhynchus).
To find out more about them, you can visit: www.rspb.org.uk
(the official website of the Royal Society for the Protection of Birds)